Effortless
WellBeing™

The Missing Ingredients
for Authentic Wellness

Evan Finer

**WELLBEING
RESOURCES**

Cover Art & Book Design by Wellbeing Resources.
Effortless Wellbeing™ is the trademark property of Evan Finer.

For information about special discount prices for bulk purchases, please contact Wellbeing Resources at the address below, or through e-mail at info@wellbeingresources.com.

Wellbeing Resources
PO Box 1117
Lake Zurich, IL 60047
www.wellbeingresources.com

First Edition
First Printing, September 2003
Second Printing, February 2004
Printed in the United States of America
ISBN 0-9743077-0-X
Library of Congress Control Number: 2003109308

With love, to Dad ...
Thank you for your love,
and showing me the way.

Table of Contents

Acknowledgments / vii
Introduction / viii
How to Use This Book / xi
Critical Preliminary Notions
    Don't Rush Progress or It Will Take Longer / 15
    Remain a Beginner, with a Beginner's Mind / 17
For Your Logical Side
    How Does Effortless Wellbeing Happen? / 21
    Looking With or Looking At You / 23
    Causing Authentic Wellbeing Effortlessly / 26
    Vibrational Perspective / 31
Three Essential Skills
    Comment on Techniques and Skills / 37
    Relaxing the Body / 39
    Learning to Breathe Again / 42
    Calming the Mind / 46
Four Essential Practices
    Comment on Skills and Practices / 57
    Sitting Still / 59
    Lying Still / 61
    Standing Still / 62
    Moving Still / 70

Common Experiences from the Practices / 72
A Few More Critical Notions
Comment on These Critical Notions / 79
On Supplemental Exercise / 80
On Eating, Drinking, and Sleeping / 84
Maintain Steadfast but Detached Intentions / 89
On Using Words and Thoughts for Wellness / 91
Maintain Integrity / 93
Create the Right Environment / 96
Maintain Focus and Be Calm / 98
Control Ego and Self-Importance / 101
Practice Acceptance and Responsibility / 104
Take as Your Advisor the Worst Case / 106
Common Barriers to Progress / 108
Training Journal
Summary of the Training Program / 115
The Journal Pages / 116
About the Author / 159
Additional Training Opportunities / 160

Acknowledgments

All those before me, the families of families that resulted in my being here, I humbly thank you. To my first and most profound teacher, Dad, I love and miss you. Thank you. To my new baby girl, Erin, my inspiration and joy, I love you. Thank you. Ellen, my wife, thank you for your love and support. I love you. Mom, you are the greatest. I love you. Thank you. I thank Bob, my stepfather, for our warm relationship. Tina, the most decent person I know and the world's best sister, thank you. I love you. Gerri, you are one-of-kind, and I love you. Tom, thank you for your kind support. I humbly thank all my teachers. Some stick in my mind. Joe Rychlak, thank you for opening my eyes to big ideas about being. Scott Baker, thank you for showing me how to make real what I thought might be possible but was elusive. Kam Yuen, thank you for sharing your profound wisdom. On an editorial and production level, I thank my wife Ellen and Marianna Zeidler. I am deeply and humbly grateful to all of you, and many others not named.

Introduction

I wrote this manuscript many years ago, because after much exploration and trial and error, I felt that I had finally put together the essential keys to becoming authentically well. I let the book sit, with occasional modification, as I continued to research and experiment. Eventually, I was convinced that this material would help people to be comfortable, happy, and optimally powerful. Moreover, I could not find any other book that contained all of the components required for authentic and effortless wellness. Books with some of the information were loaded with too much extra material, obscuring the critical information and confusing the reader. There was a clear need for a concise program like Effortless Wellbeing™. I felt compelled to help people by completing this project.

Effortless Wellbeing™ combines into a complete system the essence of the most useful, time and research tested principles and strategies for releasing and activating your inner wellness. Your wellness will accelerate, across virtually all levels of your being (physical, mental, emotional, and so on). Effortless Wellbeing™ is simple, easy-to-learn, fun, and will provide more for your personal development than you can imagine. Young, old, active, inactive, healthy, not-so-healthy, ... , it is for everyone.

This book contains all the information you need, including many insights into the various experiences you might have while following the program. In brief, you will first consider some helpful ideas about learning in general, but especially about learning Effortless Wellbeing™. Then there is an explanation for how the system works. This discussion is provided to satisfy any curiosity, but your understanding of it is not required for progress, because the training will move you toward wellness automatically. You will then learn the three essential skills of relaxing the body, breathing efficiently, and calming the mind. Next you will learn how to train these skills within the four essential practices of standing, sitting, moving, and lying down. Last, you will learn about several critical notions that will help you progress very deeply.

Interestingly, the "simple" practices of this program are also the most advanced practices there are for becoming well. Thus, Effortless Wellbeing™ training will take you as far as you wish to go with authentic wellness. You need only adhere to a schedule of roughly 30 minutes a day, four to five days per week to make substantial progress. A training journal is provided in the back of the book to help you keep track of what you are doing and how it is benefiting you. It gauges both your subjective experiences and objective data (exercises done and for how long, ratings, and so on). About five months worth of pages are provided because this should be enough to allow you to see substantial progress. If you want to continue journaling beyond this, feel free to photocopy the journal template.

It is an honor to share this valuable information with you. Please use this system and discover just how good you are at authentically being well!

How to Use This Book

This is a very concise book that contains material that has historically been highly regarded, even treasured. These are methodologies and principles to assist you in gaining deep experiential knowledge about yourself and the world.

Keep in mind that while the words of this text are easy to comprehend, some of the ideas and suggestions might not be fully comprehended initially. Some sections might seem elusive in meaning. This is because until you have gained the unique experiential knowledge from performing the various practices described, your frame of reference is limited to your past experiences and perceptual schemes. The content, if unclear at first, will become more understandable as you progress.

Ultimately, you will find that the most significant knowledge you gain will be indescribable, and can only be alluded to. Nonetheless, you'll know it when you know it, and you will be able to see your knowledge working as you improve your life.

You should read this book from cover to cover before beginning any practices. Then, as you practice, refer back every so often. You will find that when you revisit the book, it will have new meanings and implications in the same words. You might also find that something you skimmed over was significant, an essential piece of information, needed for further progress.

Critical
Preliminary
Notions

Don't Rush Progress or It Will Take Longer

The skills and practices you will learn in this book are best thought about as an art. Like an art, these skills are a unique and personal expression of yourself and are developed and refined indefinitely, through consistent and sincere training, throughout your life. Art is a journey with no real end, and so is the practice of Effortless Wellbeing™.

People often find the meaning of art difficult to grasp because modern culture emphasizes rapid progress, total understanding, and instant mastery. Meanwhile, one of the core characteristics of an art is that you cannot rush progress. Ability unfolds as you are ready and no sooner. A classic illustration of this idea resides in an often told story of a young boy who sought instruction from a master artist. The boy asked how long it would take to gain expertise. The master told the boy that it would take 15 years. The boy, displeased with the length of time required, asked how long it would take if he practiced twice as hard. The master said it would then take 30 years.

Perplexed, the boy asked how long it would take if he were to practice three times harder. The master said it would then take over 50 years. This tale underscores the reality of learning art. The more you try, or the more you obsess about achievement, the more elusive success becomes. You must appreciate and enjoy each step of the journey, remain patient, and consistently work with a focused yet gentle intention to further refine your ability, without expecting any particular result.

It is also helpful to keep in mind that progress is not always steady. There will be occasional drastic improvement, and occasional decline in progress. Over time, however, consistent effort will yield noticeable results.

Remain a Beginner, With a Beginner's Mind

In order to develop authentic wellness, or anything else, you must always maintain a beginner's mind. This is more than an open mind. An open mind is indeed helpful because it will allow you to entertain, test, and accept various profound ideas about the potential within you. But you need even less (more) than an open mind. You need an eternally childlike beginning mind, empty of ideas and expectations. You need to experience everything as though it is the first time, as purely as possible.

Like a child, you'll question, but you will not judge or omit anything based on biases. In contrast to maintaining a beginning mind, your expert mind is busy knowing, predicting, looking for, or criticizing your experiences, which results in you missing out on unique ideas, events, perceptions, and so on. The importance of forever maintaining a beginner's mind cannot be overstated. Paradoxically, you will find that this way of being will allow you to develop more than you can imagine.

For many, maintaining a beginner's mind is a great challenge. In fact, many ancient masters have said that enlightenment is easy compared to maintaining a beginner's mind. Try to maintain a beginning mind right now. Empty your mind, and consider the information and ideas in this book fully. Ask and hold questions, but suspend judgment or bias. If you think you already know what you are reading, empty your mind more and consider that perhaps something different or more extensive is being referred to.

Know that all truly great masters have worked to improve ability from this humble perspective. For example, consider the great Aikido (a Japanese martial art) founder, Uyeshiba. As a small old man, he was so highly developed that he could effortlessly throw and control many big attackers simultaneously. His ability is, and always has been, reported as truly magical. Yet, before Uyeshiba died, he said that he was just a beginner in his martial art.

For Your
Logical Side

How Does Effortless Wellbeing Happen?

You will tap into your ability to move effortlessly along an authentic path toward wellness. You will be at your absolute best with no effort. How can this be possible?

Essentially, wellness emerges from a state of simple being, where you have let go of tension, fear, worry, and so on, for long enough to truly relax. If you provide yourself with enough of an opportunity to remain in this state, you will move toward wellness, automatically. You will physically be better. You will see things more clearly. You will act with focus and purpose. You will have a good sense of yourself and how to control your life. And more!

This section provides some explanations for how the effortless wellbeing system works. It is here to satisfy that part of you that desires logical analysis. However, it is important to remember that the effortless wellbeing system will work whether you understand, believe, or even care about any of the information in this section. After all, any explanation and its underlying assumptions are necessarily only one of an infinite number of viable views. With that said, here is something for your logical side.

Looking With or Looking at You

When we seek to understand people, it is important to keep in mind that one of two main frameworks are commonly used, and each is quite distinct. On one hand, there are explanations that 'look with' a person. Alternatively, there are explanations that 'look at' a person. Each perspective is unique in how it explains the way we experience the world.

'Looking at' perspectives tend to assume that a person's experience is a direct reflection of the outside world. A person plays a minimal role in construing reality, if any. From this standpoint, my world is the same as your world, and people are explained while 'looking at' them. For example, a person who is sitting, quietly practicing effortless wellbeing exercises, can be described as having a reduced heart rate, slowed brain waves, an increased integration of left and right brain hemispheres, lowered blood pressure, increased production of beneficial hormones, decreased production of harmful hormones, and so on.

'Looking with' models tend to assume that a person plays a significant role in construing reality. Each individual has a particular way of structuring, framing, and experiencing the world. From this perspective, a person is best explained by 'looking with' her subjective eyes. Now we can describe the person who is performing effortless wellbeing exercises as favorably altering her perception of time, feeling serene, being in touch with the ebb and flow of bodily processes, feeling at one with the world, and so on. She is taking a glorious break from outside stressors. She is in her own subjective world, which makes her feel rejuvenated and vibrant.

Both perspectives are valuable for understanding effortless wellbeing. The various aspects of becoming well that can be identified 'looking at' you are useful indicators of positive, measurable states. But perhaps the most important reason for differentiating between these views is to emphasize how we must 'look with' you to find the rich experiences that we are all familiar with as living human beings. For example, if we were to exclusively 'look at' you, we might fail to notice that even something as rigid as time is alterable subjectively. You can actually elongate or shorten your experience of time, despite its external stability. You can also become proficient at creating a pleasant and meaningful experience of the world, regardless of the observable conditions in your environment.

Effortless wellbeing practice will help you to be optimally well, from the outside in, and from the inside out.

Causing Authentic Wellbeing Effortlessly

How will you cause authentic wellbeing effortlessly? Think about the meaning of 'cause' for a moment. Although causation is typically taken to mean "whatever created or brought about X," upon closer inspection there is actually much more involved. Long ago, Aristotle provided a very useful classification of the main causal schemes used throughout history. He noted that the meaning and implication of 'cause' is quite elaborate, and he described four main types of causes: material, efficient, formal, and final.

It is useful to learn about these different causal notions because it will help you to understand more broadly the means through which the effortless wellbeing system works. Thus, in this section, we will begin by gaining a basic understanding of the four causes. After that, we will discuss some ways that the effortless wellbeing system will cause your authentic wellness.

Briefly, material cause refers to the physical

substance(s) of an object, while efficient cause refers to the movement or impetus of one thing upon another, over time. It is common for people to combine material and efficient causes into a material-efficient cause, where one substance or thing acts upon on another, in a time-ordered manner. In contrast to the mechanistic material-efficient causes are formal and final causes. Formal causes are patterns, plans, or goals; and final causes are intentions. It is common for people to combine formal and final causes into a formal-final cause, where something is caused by an intention (final) to achieve a pattern or goal (formal).

Here is an example to help make sense of these causes. Suppose a person built a stereo system and you wish to understand the nature of the stereo in terms of the causes. A material cause can be the actual materials of the finished system. An efficient cause can be the movements of the creator's body in conjunction with the components (material), leading to the finished product over time. A formal cause can be the plan or blueprint used to organize the system. A final cause can be the reason the creator undertook the project in the first place, perhaps his intention to hear music.

Much can be gained from each causal understanding. Perhaps the most important reason for describing this scheme to you is that many people fail to consider the formal-final causes because our culture has focused so much on the mechanistic material-efficient causes. Though powerful in their own way, material-efficient causes do not embrace the very human idea of a cause being your intention to achieve something. In contrast, formal-final causes are based on this notion. Quite empowering, formal-final causation is independent of time and even direct spatial proximity, meaning that something in the past, present, or future can have an effect locally or distantly. I know that this can make your brain itch, but it is important to know that formal-final causes are uniquely powerful in this way.

Here is another example to help illustrate the unique power of each cause. Suppose we are at the ocean watching a sailboat moving toward an island, and we want to explain the behavior of the boat. A material-efficient based explanation can be that the waves of the water, in combination with the wind and the position of the sail, are forcing the boat to move toward the island over time. Thanks to our remarkable understanding of Newtonian physics, we can make remarkably accurate predictions based on this mechanistic approach. Now, in contrast, a formal-final based explanation can be that the boat captain intends to travel to the island and has thus positioned the sails in a manner that will aim the boat toward the island. The critical difference between the material-efficient perspective and the formal-final one is illustrated by considering this scenario one step further. What if the wind and waves change during the course of travel? Quite distinctly, the formal-final based explanation would predict that the captain will make adjustments to his sail in order to make sure that he continues to move toward the island. That is, the boat captain will make adjustments to work with his material-efficient "laws" so that his aims are achieved. What would a material-efficient position say about this issue? Only perhaps that a man on the boat moved the sails and that, again, the sail position interacting with the wind and waves, is resulting in a path toward the island.

How does the Effortless Wellbeing™ system cause your authentic wellness? A potential material-efficient cause is that performing the various practices will lead to better physical constitution and function over time, which will also have beneficial emotional and mental (and so on) manifestations. This will be effortless because the practices involved require that you do not try hard, and they do not take much time to perform. Typically, this is where causal explanations stop. However, perhaps the most important way that Effortless Wellbeing™ works is by helping you harness the vast power of your ability to intend to create a beneficial pattern within yourself and the world, which produces authentic wellness without effort. As illustrated in the boat example above, by harnessing the formal-final causes, you will gracefully work with the material-efficient constraints around you to maximize your wellness in virtually any circumstance.

Vibrational Perspective

It has been suggested that Effortless Wellbeing™ results in an acceleration of movement toward authentic wellness, along all dimensions of your being (physical, mental, emotional, spiritual, and so on). This last section is devoted to providing one explanation for how this is possible. This explanation relies on the well-respected notion that the universe can be viewed as a vast spectrum of vibrations. That is, you are a bundle of vibrations, among a mix of vibrations in the world. All aspects of yourself, your body, mind, emotions, spirit, and so on, are ultimately vibrations. In brief, the Effortless Wellbeing™ system helps you become more fluid vibrationally, and this fluidity corresponds to wellness across the various dimensions of your being.

To some, the idea that we are vibrations is hard to accept. Actually, cross-culturally, throughout history, under various names (energy, vibrations, chi, ki, prana, and so on) thinkers and scientists have embraced this idea. In particular, there are many traditions of physics, medicine, healing arts, and martial arts that are intimately linked with this perspective. If you are among those who have a hard time with this notion, consider that it is really nothing new. Light is a vibration. Sound is a vibration. X-rays are vibrations. Your cell phone transmits and receives vibrations. If you look at this paper under a high powered microscope it would reveal itself as a bunch of vibrations. All that is being said is that a vibrational analysis allows us to explain things well. It is simply one of many possible systems of explanation.

There have also been many well-respected systems of analysis of the patterns of vibrational activity within humans, animals, plants, rocks, and so on. For example, there is the meridian system, upon which acupuncture and similar treatments are based. There is the chakra system commonly embraced by yoga practitioners. There are well respected theories of networks of major and minor paths of vibrational activity, embedded within a luminous egg-like pattern of flowing vibrations. And there are many other views. The point is that for thousands of years there has been much benefit from diverse groups of people working from a vibrational perspective.

Again, the Effortless Wellbeing™ system will work regardless of whether you believe in any view, vibrational or otherwise, for how it works. However, you will note that once you begin to look at yourself and everything else vibrationally, new possibilities for being emerge. There is the potential for a deeper fluidity of self, and refined sensitivity to the vibrational experiences of everything in the world. From this perspective, it is easy to see how Effortless Wellbeing™ can produce wellness without effort. It is effortless because authentic wellness requires fluidity, and fluidity is ultimately a pure state of being, an unrestricted expression of yourself. Being truly yourself should be easy, and it will, because the simple practices of the Effortless Wellbeing™ system automatically coax vibrationally stagnant aspects of yourself back to fluidity. Moreover, you will find that the spectrum of vibrations that you are able to sense and control will expand dramatically, and you will be empowered to develop and express wellbeing more elaborately than ever before.

Three
Essential
Skills

Comment on Techniques and Skills

This section of the book will provide techniques for the development of three essential skills: relaxing the body, breathing efficiently, and calming the mind. Although these skills are related, with each one improving the others, it is useful in the beginning to develop each skill separately. Once proficiency is achieved in each, you will integrate them and they will serve as the foundation for the four practices presented in the next part of this book.

The techniques you will learn will help you immensely in developing your skill. However, it is critical to your ongoing advancement that, at some point, techniques are discarded. Techniques are like training wheels, designed to assist you in achieving a particular ability or state of being. Once skill is gained, you will perform better and advance further by freeing yourself to do whatever you feel is right. You will advance to the point of "no technique," where you intuitively know what to do and when.

But, given that you do need to start with

techniques, the benefit of using the ones described in this section is that these techniques are very pure, stripped of non-essential content and process. They are the essence of the best techniques, those used effectively around the world, for thousands of years.

Whenever possible, practice in a peaceful location where you know that you are safe and will not be interrupted. You can do or add anything that helps you relax (sounds, outdoor practice, use of scents, and so on), as long as it does not distract you. Remember that you are working toward wellness in a refined sense. Tune in to your most subtle feelings, maintain a beginner's mind, gently intend to gain ability, work consistently, and expect no particular outcome.

Most important is that you enjoy!

Relaxing the Body

You may have noticed that when you are physically tense it is difficult to remain calm or focused. One reason is that physical tension inhibits the flow of vibrations, and your thoughts and emotions reflect the fluidity of your vibrations. You will see that when you learn to relax your body it is much easier to remain centered and calm.

Below is a straightforward and very powerful exercise to help you physically relax deeply. You can perform the exercise in a variety of positions, but it is perhaps best to train lying down until you are proficient. Just take care to stay awake until you are finished.

Get comfortable lying on your back, with your eyes gently closed. Keep your legs apart slightly so that there is a small distance between your feet. Rest your arms by your sides a few inches from your body. Breathe comfortably and gently. You will be moving your attention very slowly up and down your body. Begin by focusing on and bringing your feeling attention to your feet. Spend as long as you need to feel into your feet and notice any tension. You are striving to feel very very deeply into yourself, into your vibrations, your essence. Feel the minute vibrations within your skin, bones, muscles, blood, cells, space between cells, and whatever else you can feel within your body. Notice any feelings of stagnation in the flow of vibration (tension) and dissolve it, as though melting from a solid state to a liquid and then a gas. Some people benefit from imagining tension (or "junk" that is interfering with fluidity) as being released down into the center of the earth. Some like to imagine allowing the tension to dissolve into space. Now, very slowly move the process up toward your head, attending to and feeling each section of your body, dissolving and releasing tension. As you progress up, continue to maintain and deepen the relaxation you achieved in the lower areas. By the time you get to your head, you should feel very relaxed. Nonetheless, you can always relax deeper. So, continue the process back down from your head to your feet. Then, back again from your feet to your head. And so on. Once your body is both heavy like a rock, and light like a feather, maintain and enjoy the state of relaxation for as long as you like. If you can't achieve this level of relaxation within 30 minutes, stop at that point for the day. When you get up, be sure to allow a few minutes to return to a normal state of alertness before doing any activities. Work this technique each day until you can relax with relative ease.

Learning to Breathe Again

When you were an infant, your breathing was natural and efficient. Air was effortlessly drawn down into the lower part of your lungs, filling them fully from the bottom up. You were optimally oxygenating your body. During this deep yet gentle inhale, your abdominal region expanded in all directions, softly massaging your internal organs. At just the right moment, a smooth exhale occurred, involving a natural contraction of your abdominal area, and a maximal elimination of used air. Your breathing was smooth, not forced, because your various muscles and internal organs were supple. Your breathing was not loud, but rather soft and easy. It was truly rejuvenating.

Unfortunately, at some point, you learned to breathe unnaturally. You now hold more tension, most likely with your stomach in, chest out, and shoulders back. You have learned to breathe using your chest and upper torso muscles, which requires more effort and fills only the upper portion of your lungs with air. Breathing itself now requires more of your energy, as you are meanwhile receiving less nutrients from air. Obviously, since you breathe every day, all day long, breathing poorly is a serious barrier to your wellbeing. It is critical that you train yourself to regain your once unconscious skill of proper natural (abdominal) breathing. Once you regain this ability, it will again be effortless, and you will not need to think about it.

Before discussing the procedure for learning how to breathe again, please take careful note that this is not about doing breathing exercises. This is about restoring your minute-by-minute breathing process back to its proper and efficient state. You might have heard of some of the numerous breathing exercises, for example with different pacing for the inhale–hold–exhale cycle. To be clear, many of these breathing exercises have good value. But, these are to be performed as supplemental exercises, if at all, and only after you have restored the foundation of proper abdominal breathing. Supplemental breathing exercises are not essential to the Effortless Wellbeing™ system and are therefore not presented in this book.

First, as you might guess, a relaxed and supple body will be helpful for proper breathing. So, relax. Wear loose and comfortable clothing so that your body can expand without constriction. Natural materials such as cotton are nice because they allow your skin to breathe too. As with relaxing the body, you can perform the exercise in a variety of positions, but it is perhaps best to train either lying down or sitting, until you are proficient. You can keep your eyes open or closed during this exercise, whichever works best for you. If you lie down, position yourself on your back, with your legs spread apart slightly so that there is a small distance between your feet. Rest your arms by your sides a few inches from your body. If you sit, choose any comfortable chair that allows you to maintain a relatively straight spine. Do not tilt your head too far forward or back, and do not slouch or lean backwards. Especially at first, many people find it useful to place one hand gently on the chest and one hand gently on the abdominal area so that you can easily assess whether proper internal movements are occurring.

Beginning with the inhale, draw air in gently through your nose by moving your diaphragm downward (contraction of the muscle). Your abdomen will expand outwardly, in all directions, like a balloon. The breath should sound gentle, and the sound, if any, is from the resonation of your entire respiratory system. You should not, for example, hear sound coming only from your nostrils. Your chest should be essentially motionless during this process, and your lungs will thus fill from the bottom up (the opposite of what occurs during "chest breathing"). After you have taken 75% to 80% of your air capacity, let the exhale occur, as your diaphragm relaxes back into its original position. Your abdomen will thus contract. Air travels out through your nose again.

Some people find it useful to imagine a stream of light moving down from the nose into the abdominal region on the inhale, and then flowing back out on the exhale. Some people like to imagine a balloon filling up in the abdominal area. Do what works for you. Most important is that the breathing process should not feel forced. Although you are directing it, you want to let your body breathe for you. Try to follow the breath, guiding it with as little effort as possible.

This natural method of breathing may not come easily at first, because you have forgotten it and have likely developed bad breathing habits. You might have a difficult time moving your diaphragm, expanding your abdominal area in all directions, or keeping your chest still. Just practice each day, in as relaxed a state as possible. Soon, you will be able to breathe properly and comfortably, indefinitely. Work up to at least a 15 minute training session each day until it is second nature.

Calming the Mind

The world does not necessarily need to slow down before you can have a break. You can take some time each day to slow down your mind. To those of you who have tried to calm your mind and failed, this section will help you succeed. Though it might take a while to deeply develop this skill, you will derive much benefit at each stage of your progress. Ultimately, the practice will become a source of great pleasure, and one of your most potent coping tactics. You will be able to take a mini-vacation in your mind, and while only 15 - 60 minutes tick off the wall clock, you will have a highly restorative experience with lingering benefits.

Below are the most effective methods for calming the mind. The first one mentioned involves focusing exclusively on your breathing, following your breath. This is the method I suggest you use initially, because you are currently working on breathing skill and this technique will help you improve that simultaneously. But, if you prefer, it is fine to start with any of the methods described.

At some point, be sure to experiment with all of the techniques, since they each have a unique flavor.

Most techniques involve establishing a focal point for your mind, to help keep your mind from wandering. In general, remember that if you try to force your mind into silence, it will disobey. You need to be gentle and accepting of your mind's activity, as you point the way to silence. Simply allow the thoughts to come and go, taking care not to fuel them, being sure not to create additional dialogue. Eventually, you will be able to calm your mind quickly and for long periods of time, without the use of techniques.

Practice the skill of calming your mind for at least 20 minutes a day, but remember that two minutes will help you more than nothing. You can practice in any position, but using the previously described sitting or lying position (see 'Learning to Breathe Again' section) is recommended as you begin to gain skill. You can keep your eyes open or gently closed during these exercises (unless using a visual stimulus as a focal point, such as described in 'Using External Sounds and Images'). After your session is complete, be sure to allow yourself a few minutes to return to a normal state of alertness before going about your normal activities.

Focusing on Breathing

Breathing abdominally, as you eventually always should, begin by bringing your focus exclusively to your breathing. Let go of all thoughts. Soon, of course, you will have a variety of thoughts, probably including thoughts about trying to have no thoughts. When your mind does this, relax with no worries. Acknowledge the occurring thoughts, then let them go. Do not elaborate on them. Simply and immediately refocus on your breathing. Return to hearing, feeling, and experiencing your breath completely. This technique can produce very profound experiences, aside from a silent mind state. You will find that your breathing is rather remarkable. It happens automatically, and it can be felt on a subtle level throughout your entire body. Feel the vibrations from the inhale, and from the exhale. A great deal can be learned from this simple technique.

Repeating a Word/Phrase

You can calm and focus your mind by repeating a word/phrase out loud or in your mind. This technique is frequently misunderstood. People sometimes believe that they must speak out loud during the practice. Actually, you can just mentally repeat the word/phrase. It is true that creating sound can be pleasant and help with body-mind awareness because it produces vibrations within and around the body. However, I recommend that you simply mentally repeat the word/phrase because this will help your body (mouth and tongue in particular) remain still, and thus better help your mind remain calm. Whichever method you prefer, be sure to use a word/phrase that has a calming quality for you.

Another misconception with this practice is that the word/phrase used must be based on a belief system. Actually, benefit comes from virtually any word, as long as it does not evoke a negative experience, although there is value in choosing a word/phrase that has importance to you. Important words/phrases (for example, Love, Peace, Calm, Relax, I am healthy, I am happy, and so on) are often used because they carry extra power. In a real way, a word/phrase choice organizes your experience. It sets an intention for the state you wish to achieve as your mind is calmed.

Once you have chosen a word/phrase, there are two main ways to repeat it in order to help calm your mind. One way is to simply repeat the word/phrase, over and over and over, using it as your focal point, so that thoughts are less likely to arise. Experiment with the speed of your repetitions because it will be associated with the nature of your experience. Your brain will entrain to your repetition rate. Slower brain waves (1 - 4 cycles per second) bring deep sleepy relaxation, while faster brainwaves (5 - 14 cycles per second) produce more alert states of calm. You might experience good success by starting with a fairly quick repetition rate (about 3 - 5 cycles per second mentally) and then reduce the rate to one or less repetitions per second.

A second way to use a word/phrase to calm your mind is to remain silent in your mind as long as possible, and when interrupted with thoughts, bring your attention back to the word/phrase. Then, begin a period of silence again, until you are distracted by thoughts. Then bring your attention back to the word/phrase again. Repeat this indefinitely.

Numerical Counting

Similar to the use of a word/phrase is the use of counting to assist in calming and focusing your mind. The main difference between the two approaches is that numbers do not carry as much meaning as a word/phrase. Note that I am not recommending that you count your breaths because it becomes challenging to spread the pronunciation of a number over a very long stretch of time, as when you are deeply relaxed and breathing only two or so times a minute. Again, I also do not recommend the use of counting to regulate the timing of your breathing cycle, because you are seeking to breathe automatically, at a pace that naturally reflects the state of your mind and body.

As with repeating a word/phrase, there are two techniques for counting to calm your mind. I recommend you count mentally with both methods. One way is to count repetitively, using the count as a focal point and a repetitive stimulus that entrains your brain (and thus your mind state). For example, you might start by counting one, two, three, four, over and over, at about 4 - 6 counts per second. You can then slow the pace to 1 - 2 counts per second, bringing your mind to an even calmer state.

The second method of counting involves pausing between numbers, trying to remain without thought during the gap. For example, count one and remain thoughtless. Once a thought interferes, count two, and remain thoughtless until a thought interferes again. Then count three, and so on. The goal is to remain between the numbers for as long as possible, ultimately indefinitely.

Using External Sounds or Images

External sounds or images can also be used effectively as a focal point for your mind. The word "external" is used because the stimuli are outside of your body. What is meant by sounds are things like the sound of a waterfall, rain, ocean waves, soft soothing music, and so on. What is meant by images are things like a flickering flame, spot of light, clouds in the sky, and so on. The technique involves exclusive focus on a stimulus, total immersion in it with your whole being. Like the other methods of eliminating mental chatter, when you become distracted by a thought, bring yourself back to the stimulus. If you are looking at something, relax and simply allow it to be seen and experienced. If you are listening to sounds, feel it, experience the vibrations throughout your body.

Using Internal Sounds & Sensations

You can also use as your focal point any of the various sensations occurring within you. You can attend to your heart beating, blood flowing, brain activity, and so on. You can sense it all, especially when you are silent. This is an excellent method because (like following the breath) it helps to increase your overall sensitivity to yourself and ultimately your environment. Just relax, listen and feel, without expecting anything in particular. When thoughts interfere, immediately bring your focus back to the stimulus you have chosen.

Witnessing Your Thoughts

Witnessing your thoughts is presented last because it is probably the most advanced technique in that it does not use a focal point to help prevent stray thoughts. This method of calming the mind involves the simple observation of what the mind is doing. Just watch your thoughts, without any attachment, until they stop. The idea is that by not obsessing over your thoughts, you deprive them of energy, and they stop. This is a pure and concise method. It's just you and your thoughts. You might want to start using this method as you advance toward the point of "no technique."

Four
Essential
Practices

Comment on Skills and Practices

Once you have developed reasonable ability to breathe abdominally with comfort, had a dozen or so sessions of calming your mind, and a dozen or so sessions of relaxing your body, you should integrate all of these skills into the following four essential practices. Now, your training in effortless wellbeing will be confined to deepening your skills during sitting, lying, standing, and moving. That is, once you begin with these practices, you will no longer need to work the skills independently, unless you are so inclined. Working these four practices will help you maintain a vibrant and healthy state of being, during most any activity.

This section will elaborate on the correct way to perform each practice, adding some detail to the brief descriptions of sitting and lying down that you have read previously, and explaining the standing and moving practices. It is recommended that you do one or more of these practices each day, for a total time of 30 minutes or more, five or more days per week. Make certain that each practice is performed at least once during the week. This section concludes with a discussion of some common experiences people have after performing these Effortless Wellbeing™ practices.

Sitting Still

The practice of sitting still is usually depicted elaborately, with a host of complex rules for positioning the body. This is why many people avoid it. The previous description of sitting (in the 'Three Essential Skills Section') was brief to help prevent excess concern or obsession, and to allow you to focus more on skill development. Now that you have gained skill, however, it will help to elaborate on some critical points of the optimal sitting structure.

What you have already learned is still key. Choose a comfortable chair that allows you to maintain a relatively straight spine. Do not tilt your head too far forward or back, and do not slouch or lean backward. Now, in addition, position your feet flat on the floor, parallel to each other, slightly less than shoulder width apart. Rest your hands on your thighs, in your lap, or by your sides, whichever is most relaxing. Position your head in such a way that it feels weightless and rests easily. Try imagining a string pulling your crown upward, bringing your chin in slightly, resulting in a gentle straightening of your neck. Depending, of course, on your body structure, your ears will be lined up closer to the center of the shoulders than the front. As if you were sitting on the edge of a stool, refine the position of your lower back so that it is straightened more, lessening the s-curvature. Once you feel that you have set yourself properly, rock gently forward and back, and settle into what feels like the center. Then, rock gently side to side, and again settle into what feels like the center. Now breathe abdominally, relax physically, and calm your mind. A session of 20 - 30 minutes will produce excellent results.

(I again emphasize that the key is to be comfortable, with your spine as straight and vertical as possible. You want to be able to relax fully, without falling over.)

Lying Still

The practice of lying down is probably the easiest for most people. The positioning is straightforward and it is relatively easy to surrender to gravity while lying down. As described previously, start by lying on your back. You can keep your eyes open or closed. Maintain a small distance between your feet and legs. You might want to try different arm positions from session to session. One day, for example, place your arms by your sides a few inches from your body. Another day, try resting your hands over your abdominal area with a small space between them. Another day, try positioning your hands in a similar fashion but over your chest. When comfortable, begin to breathe abdominally, relax your body, and calm your mind). A 15 - 30 minute session will produce great benefits. Do not fall asleep!

Standing Still

The benefits of standing still in the manner described below are extremely profound. It is an ancient secret for developing health and physical power. It is rare that a teacher/author knows of and thus prescribes standing practice. And, if it is offered, it rarely receives the emphasis it deserves as one of the most important exercises a person can perform. Despite this lack of general awareness, the very best teachers, those who have remarkable knowledge and profound skill — the best Olympic trainers, martial arts masters, masters of healing arts, and so on — are well aware of the following standing practice. They consider it to be the bread and butter of training, the "this is the secret, do it at the expense of all else" sort of practice.

Through the practice of standing you will clear tensions and restore fluidity to your entire being, on all levels (physical, mental, emotional, spiritual, and so on). You will develop body unity, great physical strength, and overall power. Your ability to stand and move efficiently will be amplified greatly, as you learn how to surrender to gravity while maintaining a vertical relationship with the earth. You will also become more sensitive to the subtle vibrational currents within and around you. Consistent practice of standing, even for short 10 - 15 minute sessions a few times a week, will transform and energize you far beyond your expectations.

Although there are a variety of beneficial standing postures, you will learn the essential position (see illustration, p.62), and will benefit from using this stance indefinitely. To begin, stand naturally, with your arms by your side, and make the following adjustments. Place your feet parallel to each other with the distance between them a bit less than the width of your shoulders. Bend your knees so that they are just past being unlocked, but not so far that your knees extend beyond your toes. Roll your arms and shoulders slightly forward so that your palms face backward. In order to maintain as vertical a spine as possible, keep the crown of your head gently raised by imagining it being pulled gently from above by a string. This will straighten the back of your neck somewhat, gently bringing your chin in. Tuck your buttocks forward, though not forcefully. This adjustment should occur naturally when you unlock your knees, if you are relaxed. The effect is that the s-curve in the lower back is straightened. Now, both at your neck and your lower back areas, you are gently straightening the spine. Most important is that you relax as much as possible. In the beginning, maintaining the proper positioning can be a bit uncomfortable. However, it will eventually become very comfortable, and it will allow you to stand without using too much muscle strength (tension).

Stand for a minimum of ten minutes a day in the beginning. If you are like most people, you will discover that it is quite difficult. Don't become discouraged. Even strong, well-conditioned athletes are challenged initially. View the difficulty of this seemingly simple exercise as validation of its significance. You will probably begin to tremble or have other interesting sensations. This happens to many people and is OK as long as you are not in pain. The following section 'As You Progress With Standing,' will talk more about some common experiences people have. Over time, you will develop the ability to maintain stillness and deep relaxation while you stand. Increase the amount of time consistently, but comfortably, until you can stand for 30 minutes.

The practice of standing is often called 'standing like a tree' because of the various similarities. A tree is stable, with roots planted deep in the ground. When a person is relaxed and standing still, he too is firmly connected to the ground, "planted" without resistance. A tree has a body above the earth, effortlessly reaching upward, drawing nourishment from the ground. So too is the upper body of a standing person effortlessly drawn upward, nourished and powered by the earth's vibrations and the rebound from the compression of the relaxed lower body into the earth. Perhaps most importantly, the tree and a standing person are both naturally at peace, supple yet stable. Think about and elaborate on this comparison over time, as you progress with the practice.

As You Progress with Standing ....

After you have had many sessions of standing, you will probably notice various changes in the way you experience the practice. On one hand, it is good if you do not know what to expect because it helps to insure that you will not inadvertently interfere with what happens. On the other hand, some of the experiences you might have will be perplexing if you have no idea about what is common. In favor of the second concern, while respecting the first, below are some, but not all, experiences you might have. Be careful not to look for or create these experiences, because if you do, you might miss what is actually happening. It is possible that you will not even have the experiences as described.

Trembling or Shaking. In the early stages of training, after ten minutes or so you might experience trembling, or even pronounced shaking. In extreme instances, people literally bounce on the ground. If this happens, stop for the day. Trembling is a sign of progress in a sense, because it is the result of your internal processes and circulation (various vibrations) being activated and working hard to flow better while being blocked by tension. However, trembling is something you will work to eliminate. Though paradoxical, the way to eliminate trembling is to relax into it, rather than to resist it with additional tension. Over time, as you become less tense and more fluid, with less restriction to the flow of vibrations, trembling will stop.

Heat and Sweat. Particularly during the early stages of training, you might become very warm or hot. You might also sweat heavily. In some ways, this is a sign of progress, indicating that your internal circulation (vibrations) is more active; but, it is still indicative of too much tension (resistance), resulting in excess heat. Like a frayed wire runs too hot from electricity, your body is still a less-than-perfect conductor of energy (vibrations) and will run too hot. The more fluid you become, the less intense the heat and sweat will be. While working through the shaking described in the previous section, you will probably get warm or hot. Once you get past the trembling, you will have less of a problem with excess heat. Eventually, you will be warm while standing, but without profuse sweating and excessive heat.

Refined Vibrations. Typically, once you can stand still with reasonable comfort, you will begin to notice fine vibrations in at least some parts of your body. Now you will begin to have some experiential knowledge about what I have been calling 'vibrations.' Often these are experienced as a buzzing sensation, or an electric feeling. Sometimes there is a pulsing aspect to the vibrations, like big waves of a fine vibrating current. Many find this experience pleasurable, but at first it can be remarkable and different from anything you have experienced within your own body. Again, don't try to create or augment this sensation, just notice it and let it be. Like most sensations, it will come and go, eventually giving rise to something new and perhaps even more interesting.

Distinct Vibrational Patterns. Eventually, you will experience the presence of vibrations not only within but also around your body. Within you, the vibration feelings will move around. And, most likely to your absolute amazement, you will begin to distinctly feel the presence of vibrations outside of your body. It will probably be different than anything you can recall experiencing, but think of it as being similar to the way heat emanates from a hot mug of coffee. Your subtle vibrations ripple beyond your physical body, like the way waves of water ripple a large distance past the source that initiated them. Basically, you are becoming more vibrant, and you can sense it better. Be sure to maintain your beginner's mind, expect nothing in particular, and enjoy these amazing aspects of standing still.

Concluding Comment on Likely Experiences. The preceding descriptions are more extensive than most I have seen written, but keep in mind that the process forever evolves, is different for each person, and is ultimately not easily described. As a general guiding principle, do not worry about what you experience, unless you are in pain or otherwise distressed. The standing exercise, though it involves no gross external movement, is providing a rigorous internal workout. Combined with your increased ability to calm and relax your mind, you are going to have all sorts of wonderful experiences. Perform each session as though it is a brand new and instructive experience, providing something interesting and useful to help you become more fluid and healthy.

Moving Still

In addition to being able to relax, breathe efficiently, and calm your mind while sitting, lying, and standing, you must also work on maintaining these qualities while moving. This is actually the way true masters perform various movement arts. I recommend that you practice with walking (actually a fairly common application) because you are familiar with the mechanics. This will be a challenge, but it will elevate your wellness and personal power to a greater level. Little by little, you will gain the ability to move in a calm and relaxed state with a unified body. You will perform physical tasks more optimally, and gain remarkable insights into your body and how it moves.

This is not like the type of walking you do for a cardiovascular workout, or the type that you do in general. This is slow, deliberate walking, about 1 - 10 steps per minute. Initiate the process by first standing for a few minutes, as described in 'Standing Still,' and then slowly bring a leg forward without losing the deep connection to the ground you have established. Use minimum muscular strength to move your leg. Feel the leg you move become empty while the other leg becomes full. Place the lifted/moved leg back down, let it fill up again, as you move the other leg. Relax, relax, relax. Listen to your body, allow it to do what it needs, naturally. Feel inside and outside of yourself as you walk. Feel and "listen" to the ground. Take your time.

This practice can, like sitting, be over analyzed. Don't worry too much about the details, as long as you follow the above guidelines you will gain ability and benefit. You might want to practice this in a secluded area where you will not be interrupted. Walk for 5 - 15 minutes a session. Because this is a difficult practice, remember to practice without obsession or worry, with a beginner's mind, and with a gentle intention to gain ability.

Common Experiences from the Practices

One of the most challenging aspects of teaching the essential practices of Effortless Wellbeing™ is trying to help you move in the right direction, while not giving too much detail about what your experience will be like. As described previously regarding the common outcomes of standing practice, it is almost a necessity to keep you in the dark somewhat because while many manifestations of the journey you are embarking on are common, there is an unmistakable uniqueness for each person. Thus, there is a danger in providing too much information because it could confuse you, reduce your ability to maintain a beginner's mind, and stop your progress as you wait for something that will never come as described. Ancient wisdom has in fact suggested that the knowledge that can be described is not the eternal or most true. Nonetheless, I think you will benefit from a brief discussion of a few issues that are not likely to distract your progress. It is my hope that informing you of the following information will help you to stay with the training, by underscoring some things that might have confused you. I also hope to provide you with extra motivation by describing some exciting experiences you will likely have. The issues addressed in the remainder of this section are cleansing-healing reactions, discovering the "I (you)" behind what you thought was the "I (you)," beginning to experience vibrations or subtle sensations, and feeling more deeply.

Cleansing - Healing Reactions

It is often perplexing to practitioners that there is sometimes a brief period of feeling worse, along a variety of dimensions (physical, emotional, mental, and so on), after undertaking these practices. Often called a cleansing-healing reaction, this occurrence is usually attributed to old "junk" being cleared out of your system, causing a disturbance as it works its way out. Most cleansing-healing reactions are not that bad. Consider a few examples. People who have a tendency to suppress their emotions, like anger or resentment, might have these emotions resurface as a result of becoming more relaxed. They might need to process these old issues before they can develop further. For some, professional treatment is appropriate. For most, the issues will be resolved quickly and easily, especially given that they are improving their overall wellness. Some examples of physical cleansing-healing reactions are feeling somewhat tired, or having what seems like a cold, or having old injuries act up for a while. This can be explained as a result of the more relaxed and supple body tissues releasing trapped "toxins". In general, there are a variety of experiences that could occur, like vivid dreams, old thoughts resurfacing, mild emotional swings, and so on. Of course, if you are ever concerned, see the appropriate professional (medical doctor, psychologist, and so on) because there is always a chance that something worthy of treatment is going on. For most people, however, it is just a few bumps on the path to purification. Know that many before you have gone through it, and things will be better. Of course, in life, there will always be periods of healing and learning that continue to emerge indefinitely.

Finding the You Behind the You

An exciting experience you will likely have, after diligently performing the practices, is that you will find there is a "you (I)" behind what you thought was the "you (I)". For example, as you begin to calm your mind and watch your thoughts, it will become experientially clear that your relationship to your thoughts is different than you thought. You are not simply your thoughts. It is almost comical to begin to gain the ability to watch the things your mind throws at you when you detach and let it happen. Similarly, as you gain ability to sense your body on a subtle level, you will notice that there is more to you than your body. This is the stage where you will start to get closer to what is often called unconscious material, and you will begin to reclaim your power as the creator of the content of your mind in particular and your world in general. This is an interesting turning point, and you will continue to be amazed from here forward.

Experiencing Vibrations or Subtle Sensations

Another exciting aspect of this training is that you will begin to unmistakably experience new and very subtle sensations. You will feel and sense things happening within your body and the vibrational field around it. People, plants, rocks, electronic devices, pets, food, ... , everything can be experienced subtly. Initially, you might not know exactly how to interpret these new sensations. Just take note of the various experiences that you have, when, where, and so on. Eventually, you will notice patterns and begin to make sense of it, in the same way that you have come to know hot, cold, mean, nice, fun, scary, and so on. You will especially need your beginner's mind now to keep on learning.

Feeling Deeply, Both Good and Not-So-Good

Once you are more sensitive to subtle sensations, more in tune to yourself and your surroundings, you might find that the scope and intensity of your feelings is amplified. In general, this is a blessing, and will improve your intuition, empathy, and ability to make good decisions for yourself. You will find that many things you previously never noticed are exquisitely rich. But there is a flip side. You might also feel more deeply in response to a friend's pain, or you might be more bothered by the vibrational emissions of your cell phone, and so on. Some people feel the need to make adjustments in their life because things that did not bother them before, do bother them now. Overall, you will probably prefer being more sensitive, having this additional information about yourself and the environment. This is certainly nothing to fear because it is always possible to revert back to a less sensitive self if you desire (humans are great at learning to deny, suppress, and ignore feelings).

A Few More
Critical Notions

Comment on These Critical Notions

The essential way for you to continue to evolve with effortless wellbeing is to perform the integrated practices as described. Make a commitment to yourself to use the Effortless Wellbeing™ system because the benefits will be worth it, beyond what you imagine.

As you diligently perform the practices, you will benefit from integrating the following critical notions. They, like the essential practices, are derived from the very best cross-culturally and historically effective ideas for maximizing your wellness. Like most profound ideas, they are simple. It is also probable that you will begin to use most of these suggestions automatically, as a result of your consistent training with the essential practices, because these critical notions are associated with a calm, pure state of being.

On Supplemental Exercise

It is well accepted that a few hours of brisk cardiovascular exercise each week is good for your health. I recommend, at a minimum, that you take several 20 - 30 minute brisk walks each week in addition to your Effortless Wellbeing™ training, taking care to relax and breathe properly. Walking is a great way to gain the benefits of exercise without undo stress on your body.

If, rather than walking, you want your cardiovascular workout to include "harder" exercises, such as weight training, tennis, basketball, wrestling, and so on, you can and should perform these sports while maintaining proper breath control, relaxation, and good mental focus. It is somewhat difficult at first, but if you persist and succeed in integrating these skills into your sports, it will result in peak performance. Ask any highly developed athlete, even power weightlifters, and they will tell you that in order to perform optimally, they adhere to principles of proper breathing, tension reduction, and focusing.

But you don't have to be a professional to

perform optimally. One of my favorite and first observations of relaxed, effortless power in sports was when my father entered a softball throwing contest at a large public picnic. I was about 8 years old. My two sisters, my dad, and I were watching the contest. My dad was commenting on the performance of the participants. He said much of what I had heard him say before, including ideas that he had demonstrated for me on a small backyard scale. As we watched big men take a running start, flex big muscles, make grunting noises, and throw the ball great distances, he said things like "he's trying too hard;" "he's not using his body well;" "tensing like that won't help him;" and so on. I had always trusted my dad's teachings about effective performance, but I thought these guys were incredible. "Maybe I'll give it a try," he said. My sisters and I were a bit concerned. First of all, my dad was a relatively small man, about 5' 6" and 145 pounds. The other contestants were much bigger. He had also just barely recovered from an injury that required surgery. I was worried that he was going to embarrass himself, and I prepared to feel sorry for him. He quietly stood in line, as I dreaded the moment that he would "try it." Finally, the last participant, my dad was given the softball. He held if for a moment, gazed into the sky, and gently bounced up and down. His demeanor of calm and physical relaxation was so different from everyone before him that my sisters and I, and everyone else watching, were perplexed. He took a few easy steps, and released the ball so gracefully that I thought my fears were realized. To my literal shock, the full-sized softball was propelled as if from a cannon. It disappeared into the sky in a beautiful arc, significantly farther than any other. My sisters and I were beside ourselves with admiration and awe. Spectators looked confused. My dad thought nothing of it.

Regardless of what you prefer for your cardiovascular program, begin to think of exercise as a means to gain energy, rather than to deplete it. Many people, with the best health improvement intentions, begin an exercise program with workouts that absolutely exhaust them, pushing their bodies beyond the limit. They believe they have done good. Actually, they have drained themselves of energy and will likely cause more harm than good. It is true that many well-coached athletes and other well-informed people properly use the technique of overload. But, most who exercise this way do so regularly, without adequately rest between sessions, leading to sickness or physical injury. For most, this is then the beginning of the end of what could be a valuable, life-long relationship with gentle, regular exercise.

When you supplement your training with additional exercise, regardless of what type, you want to work at a level where the exercise is enjoyable for nearly all of its duration (80% - 100%), with perhaps on some days, a few spurts of extra effort. You should be able to comfortably carry on a conversation while exercising, and your heart should not "beat out of your chest." Do not worry about how much you can do, or how fast you can do it. You will improve over time and will be able to do more, comfortably. It has been shown time and again that you will gain more ability (fitness) if you train properly, as described above. You cannot rush progress.

On Eating, Drinking, and Sleeping

The way you eat, drink, and sleep has a definite effect on your wellness and overall energy level. These disciplines are complicated, and the related information is vast. This section will briefly discuss some basic but important guidelines, common to many wellness programs, but not necessarily well known. Of course, before trying any new ideas in these areas, you should consult with your doctor.

Regarding what you eat, you will benefit from reducing consumption of processed, "fast," and otherwise unhealthy foods in favor of freshly prepared foods. The availability of organic foods (fresh and fresh-frozen) is expanding and the prices are coming down. If affordable, you might want to think about consuming these foods as a means to limit pesticide and other toxic ingredients. Include enough "live" foods in your diet, such as raw vegetables and fruit. Try to drastically reduce consumption of refined sugar, a notoriously harmful substance for a variety of reasons. There is plenty of naturally occurring sugar in healthy foods (fruit, and so on). Be sure you eat enough "good fats." An emphasis is often placed on reducing fat, without enough care to make certain that consumption of necessary fat is maintained. Experts recommend integrating olive oil, flax seed oil, and fish oils into your diet. You still want to consume a minimum of the more harmful saturated fats. If you are pressed for time, try hard to think of a creative way to eat healthy in a hurry. Many restaurants, and even "fast food" chains, are offering better choices. If you really want to, you can manage something significantly better than garbage.

Regarding how much you eat, there is good evidence to suggest that you will benefit from limiting the amount of food you eat to only what you need, which is probably a lot less than you think. Listen to your body and its hunger signals and do not eat unless you need to. (Good luck, right? Try your best!) Importantly, this is not a diet tip, although you will certainly become leaner. The reason for this suggestion is that the process of digestion requires a lot of energy. Most of us who have binged occasionally know the fatigue that results from the body working overtime to digest too much food. In brief, we want to maximize our energy gain from food by eating just enough to fuel ourselves, but not so much that we lose energy as a result of excessive digestion. There may be even more than energy to gain from eating less. Animal research has shown a direct relationship between food consumption and lifespan. Animals on restricted calorie diets live substantially longer than animals on a normal eating program, and are much more active while alive. Not everyone likes to draw conclusions about humans based on animal research, but this is good food for thought. In addition to eating only what you need, you might also want to investigate the benefits of performing occasional short-term fasts. There is good evidence and a long tradition to suggest that, properly executed, a fast assists in healing the body, clearing the mind, and even invigorating the spirit. Of course, be certain to check with your doctor before trying a fast. And, be sure to start with small ones (a meal, or a day) before doing anything longer. Ideally you should work with someone who knows about the practice and can monitor your response.

In addition to what and how much you eat, the way that you combine foods affects energy levels, regardless of the amount eaten, because some foods work better together in the digestion process than others. In fact, some foods are said to directly interfere with one another during digestion. The more you can limit the energy requirements of digestion, while being certain to receive adequate nutrition, the more you conserve your power. It is beyond the scope of this book to go into details, but if you are interested, it is worthwhile to investigate current wisdom on developing an eating program that takes food compatibility into account. You will probably be very surprised to find that some combinations you have been eating for years are challenging for your digestion system. (For example, a steak with a potato is said to be a bad choice because protein and starch counter each other during digestion.) Finally, limit your fluid intake both thirty minutes before and after eating, because excess fluid can prolong digestion.

Now with the basics of eating covered, the issue of fluid consumption should be addressed. It is very important that you drink enough throughout the day and evening, water being the best. Recommendations for how much to drink vary, and depend on your weight and how active you are. Most sources say to start with about 60 - 80 ounces of water a day. Recently, there has been some debate about the amount, but the dissenters stand in the face of a long tradition. Given that your body is comprised primarily of fluid, it makes sense to keep it nicely hydrated. Experiment with the amount that is best for you, but do not underestimate the importance of drinking enough fluids, ideally pure water.

What if you do not maintain a perfect eating plan? What about supplements? There is a big trend lately (mid-to-late 1990s) toward using supplements (vitamins, minerals, herbs, and so on) to provide nutrients not received from food. Although they can be helpful if used properly, I recommend that you exercise caution with supplements. Too much can be harmful, and there is reason to believe that your body cannot utilize many of the available supplement formulations. If you feel a need to use supplements, it is worth your time and money to consult with a professional nutritionist, in coordination with your doctor, to help determine what, if any, supplementation would help you. Theoretically, you can learn about this on your own, but there is a tremendous variety of supplements, and a massive amount of associated propaganda.

And be sure to get enough sleep. Especially in our current social climate, we are constantly on the go, squeezing more and more into each day. Many people are not getting enough rest, and this is a serious problem because it is during sleep that our body restores and rejuvenates. Make a commitment to yourself to get enough sleep.

Maintain Steadfast but Detached Intentions

You participate and create in the world not only with overt behaviors, but also with your intentions. Currently, you might do so loosely or even unknowingly, but intentions can be deliberately and effectively used to assist in manifesting wellbeing and more. In the beginning, this will be somewhat difficult, but soon it will be easy. This is because the successful use of intending is related to your skill with calming your mind, relaxing your body, and breathing properly, the outcomes of your ongoing Effortless Wellbeing™ training.

You can release an intention in a single burst, in the calm silent mind state while you are performing practices, and you can also gently maintain an intention indefinitely. I recommend you do both. Well executed, an intention spreads all of the necessary information (vibrations) throughout the universe to create a complex pattern of activities, thoughts, events, and so on, that help to create what you desire. Initially, you might invoke your five senses to intend: see it, feel it, smell it, hear it, taste it; create the experience in your imagination. Over time, the quality of your intending will change, and increase in power substantially. You will intend with your entire being, naturally. Eventually, you will not easily be able to describe the way you intend, or what it feels like when you do it right.

A critical ingredient to the successful use of intending is that you do not attach to or obsess over the outcome. There are numerous reasons why you benefit, but the main one is that if you attach or obsess you will be holding back energy from the process. Remember, thoughts and emotions, such as attachment or obsession, use a lot of energy. Thus, if you are thinking and fearing and worrying, you and your intentions will have less power. You need to literally release your intentions, letting them work with maximum power.

On Using Words and Thoughts for Wellness

Sometimes referred to as "affirmations" or "positive thinking," you might have had some experience with the practice of using words and thoughts to create wellness. If you are like most people, you used a variety of empowering phrases, over and over. Most likely, it did not work and you were annoyed with the whole thing by the time you gave it up. Unfortunately, most people are not instructed on the proper way to use words and thoughts for wellness, and therefore spin their wheels.

In short, the critical component for effectively using empowering words and thoughts for wellness is that you think or say the affirmations in the calm silent mind state. Otherwise you are just adding more noise to your mind's chatter. When done properly, using thoughts and words during your calm mind state can yield nice benefits. One of the techniques I recommended for calming the mind makes use of words and thoughts as a focal point for your mind. The benefit is that once you achieve some inner silence, your choice of words or thoughts does affect your wellness. For example, you can use "I am healthy", or "I am flexible" or "I am stronger each day," and so on.

Experiment with this methodology and use it as often as you like. In the long term, however, as I stressed before, I recommend that you work toward eliminating techniques. Instead of repeating words and phrases, use the more pure expression of your desires: your intention. As described previously (see 'Maintain Steadfast but Detached Intentions'), when you intend, it is a vibrational expression of your entire being, released into the universe to help organize the world in a manner that supports your wishes.

Maintain Integrity

This discussion is related to two meanings for the word 'integrity'. One meaning refers to wholeness or unity. The other is related to the idea of goodness or morality. It is worthwhile to maintain integrity in both senses of the word.

In terms of being whole or unified, the applications and benefits are vast. Physically, you will develop more unity from the essential practices you are performing (especially standing and moving), and great gains in your physical efficiency and power will result. On other levels, such as your personality and its associated behaviors, you will find that you are better and stronger the more consistent you are. For example, if you are devoted to your health and wellness, it will torment you, and drain your personal resources (energy, enthusiasm, and so on), to work in a highly polluted environment, or smoke tobacco, or eat junk food. Or, for example, if you consider yourself to be a kind person, and behave that way in the main, an occasional vulgar outrage at a fellow driver on the road will detract from your fluidity of being. Keep this meaning of personal integrity in mind, hold a gentle intention to improve, and consistently work to eliminate the poisonous contradictions in your life. You might notice issues popping up in a variety of areas.

In terms of being a good person, both with yourself and others, integrity will yield big improvement in your wellbeing. Respect yourself and others. Give to yourself and others gifts of love, acceptance, appreciation, and in some cases even a meal, money, or whatever you feel is appropriate. You can even say something nice to someone silently if you are uncomfortable or if otherwise restricted. On a vibrational level, the gift will be transmitted and received. (Have you ever been with someone and felt warmth in your heart?) Forgive yourself and others for wrong doings, for not being perfect. Don't fight with yourself or others. Rather, engage in meaningful and productive dialogue geared toward understanding and cooperation. If this is not possible, turn the other cheek and walk away.

All of these suggestions for goodness are "Golden Rules," the sorts of ideas that you would teach a child. How can you argue with that? Well, you might say that in some situations a person does not deserve respect. Or, in some situations a person cannot be forgiven. In some situations you have to fight. Indeed, at times these seem like viable arguments. Nonetheless, as a general program of being in and enhancing the world, seek to behave according to these ideals.

Numerous explanations can be proposed to explain how maintaining integrity, in both senses of the word, can improve your wellness and personal power. Some would say that through behaving with goodness, you are alleviating feelings of indebtedness to the world, which are draining. Some would say that you are sending good vibrations into the world and this rebounds back and empowers you. Some would say that you are eliminating the unhealthy subconscious and conscious guilt that results from mistreating others or from being personally inconsistent. Regardless of the explanation you like, if any, behaving with integrity will help you feel better about yourself, others, and the world.

Create the Right Environment

An important point to make following the above guidelines for behaving with integrity, is that there are some people, places, things, and so on, that are aversive and we do not need to deal with them. Of course, as much as possible, make your environment pleasant and energizing. Polluted air is no good for you, so try to avoid it. Set up an air purification system in your home to keep the air you breathe as clean as possible. Avoid people with bad intentions. Just because you should turn the other cheek when confronted by an unsavory person does not mean that you should welcome him or her into your home. Surround yourself with nice people, plants (helps clean the air, and more), pleasant smells (flowers, essential oils, and so on), pleasant music, and anything else that truly makes you feel good, happy, and energized. Importantly, listen to yourself and make authentic choices. Just because classical music pleases many people does not mean it will please you. Avoid falling into the trap of doing what is stereotypically pleasant, or what other people say you should do. Only you know what is energizing for you. As you progress in your training, and your sensitivity is heightened, you will easily make authentic choices for your environment because some people, places, and things will feel right.

Many people also find it energizing to eliminate from their environment those things that are not pleasant and also no longer needed. That is, clear the "clutter". But, this does not mean that you cannot have areas with a lot of things. My father-in-law's workshop/garage, over 30 years, has developed a most unique personality as a result of the careful collection and placement of literally thousands of items. Everything has a memory, story, or personal meaning. My father-in-law is very happy and energized in his workshop and I would not recommend he throw out anything. Basically, you want to keep what you truly want and need but get rid of the rest. If you are a habitual buyer, begin to ask yourself if you really want what you are buying. Will it give you pleasure? If the object you are considering for purchase will not truly please you, then why bother increasing meaningless clutter.

Maintain Focus and Be Calm

Scattered thoughts, emotional strain, physical tension, and improper breathing all rob you of energy. These are important reasons why you should perform the essential practices, learning to breathe properly, calm your mind, and relax your body. You will also benefit from maintaining these states all the time, with some modification. For example, during daily activities it is not always possible or appropriate, to maintain a completely silent mind because you are doing things. However, you can maintain a supple body, proper breathing, and mentally focus on the present events exclusively. This will foster the occurrence of optimal performance and remarkable experiences.

Sometimes called being in the "flow" or the "zone," you may have had an experience like this, where you were acutely in touch with what you were doing, and nothing more. You performed at a vastly superior level than normal. Your perception of time and space were different than normal. Upon returning from this state, you needed a moment to reflect upon what transpired, to consider it with your non-zone mind. While most people have one or two good examples, the best professional athletes and performers virtually rely on the zone state to remain a cut above the rest.

Consider for clarification an example of peak performance in the zone. A weekend basketball player with average skill, in the span of a few seconds, had an experience in a game that seemed like minutes. He was running towards the basket when a teammate passed him the ball. After the catch, he experienced an unshakable connection with the basket. He said, "everything was simple. A person was here, so I went there ... another defender was here, so I went over there. The basket was huge, just waiting for me. I couldn't miss. It was easy, and I had all of the time in the world. It's hard to describe what it was like." Actually, he had scored under very complicated and difficult conditions, and was heavily fouled. To him, it was easy, because he was performing in a pure and focused state.

The good news is that you can increase the occurrence of zone states by consistently working with the Effortless Wellbeing™ practices and gently integrating the skills (breathing, relaxing, mental calm and focus) into your day-to-day activities. Eventually, you will effortlessly perform at your best, in the zone, much more frequently, and across a variety of situations (work, love, play, and so on).

Control Ego and Self-Importance

The idea of controlling ego and self-importance is not as straightforward as it sounds. There are so many levels to this suggestion that volumes could be devoted to it, without fully conveying its depth. On the other hand, it is simple. I will convey these ideas as simply as possible. Rest assured that if you do not grasp this initially, you will gain a deeper understanding over time, even better than can be expressed in words, as you progress with your training.

Basically, the idea is that to be truly fluid internally, and in relation to the world, you should break down the imaginary barrier between yourself and the world. What does ego have to do with that? First, when you think of the meaning of ego, you might take it to mean being full of yourself, believing you are wonderful, and so on. Actually, this common way of using the word is not the topic of discussion. Ego, for our purposes, means your self boundaries or self definitions, both those that you consciously embrace and those that silently guide

101

you. Using this meaning, reducing ego refers to allowing yourself to be, authentically, without any constraints from self boundaries.

Theoretically, on a vibrational level, you are literally one with the world. There is no break in the relationship between your vibrations and those around you. Everything flows together. By not forcing a separation between your self and everything else, you will be more in touch with, and able to maintain a more symbiotic relationship with, everything. This is one of the big ideas driving the many wellness programs that recommend reducing ego. This idea is also related to the well known prescription for wellness that states, "be one with everything."

A useful way of helping you reduce ego is working to reduce self-importance. Critically, this does not mean that you are supposed to think of yourself as insignificant. You are quite significant, an expression of the entire universe. Similarly, this does not mean that you are supposed to let people take advantage of you, or let people abuse you. Rather, the idea is that self-importance requires maintaining a firm self definition or self boundary (ego), and reducing it helps you dissolve the self-world barrier. People often get a better sense of this suggestion by considering the following questions. What would you gain if you were not so worried about how important you are? If you are slighted by someone, would you be as troubled or angered? If an untrue rumor about you is spread would this disturb you as much? Would you believe that you are less significant than another person who has a better paying job? In short, would you be wasting energy thinking and worrying about things that might not matter and that you ultimately cannot control?

Reducing self-importance and ego is, according to many traditions, one of the greatest things you can do to boost your personal power and energy because so much energy is wasted upholding the boundaries of and the importance of the self, both to others and to the self. Gently carry the intention to reduce your self-importance and ego. Ask yourself frequently how self-importance and ego are affecting you and your relationships. Paradoxically, you will feel better about yourself and others as a result.

Practice Acceptance and Responsibility

To practice acceptance is to appreciate and accept that the world is intricately and intelligently ordered. The idea is that as a dynamic system, the universe is whole and complete, with each part being an integral and symbiotic component of the whole. From this perspective, you are freed from a mechanistic and rigid interpretation of the situations in which you find yourself. It is possible to view your current situation ("good" or "bad") as part of a meaningful and necessary aspect of the world order. By accepting that your life is as it needs to be, according to a grand order that you cannot entirely comprehend or control, you can better relax and enjoy your unpredictable journey. You will be able to better accept that you cannot always forcefully control your environment through simple plans and step-by-step, cause-effect behavior sequences. You will appreciate, and view with more awe, the natural twists, turns, ebbs and flows.

But how can you take responsibility for creating

or participating in this complex system? Well, you will no longer try to micro-manage or force outcomes, instead you will gently intend for what you desire, and work consistently without compulsion or strong attachment. As you plan, strategize, and perform, you will now find opportunities and options more readily, and these options will meet less resistance in the world. You will actually be stepping up to a higher, less mechanistic level of creating what you desire. And, as events unfold, you will practice acceptance, not criticizing or questioning how or when things happen. You will trust the order of the universe and its ability to integrate and organize your intentions and actions into the grand scheme. There will be a flexible quality to your experience, and you will tend to feel your way more than think your way. As a result of your training, you will be more authentic and fluid and thus flow more comfortably and successfully in the dynamic world system.

As with many of the profound ideas and practices, you might not have a comfortable grasp on this until your knowledge is based on experience. Once you see how these ways of being work for you, it will become clear just how powerful they are.

Take as Your Advisor the Worst Case

When things are not going as you would like, and even when they are, it is useful to consider a worse case scenario. Many traditions go so far as to take this recommendation to the extreme of always remembering the fact that death is a certainty. This will help you stay on the path of acceptance, and also help you remain truly thankful for what you have. It will help you live each moment to the fullest.

Granted, this is not always easy. When you feel sorry for yourself because you can barely pay your bills, it is not always easy to take comfort in knowing that you could be living on the street, in the cold, with no home. When you are sad because you have an injury, it is not always easy to take comfort in knowing that you could have worse damage. But, it is true that things can always be worse, and it is beneficial to contemplate this during your weaker moments.

A great way to practice this idea further is to

consider death to be your personal advisor. Think of death as being always near you, that you are walking with death. When life is tough, ask death how you are doing. Ask just how bad things are. Listen for the answer. Investigate the usefulness of this compelling and experientially beneficial method. It is more powerful than the purely cognitive approach of telling yourself, "it can always be worse...."

Common Barriers to Progress

Now that you have been exposed to the practices for developing yourself along a variety of powerful dimensions, it is up to you to practice. Although reading the training procedures and the various ideas is necessary and instructive, you will gain little from only reading the material. You need to practice, consistently, with detachment, and a beginner's mind, in order to gain the benefits and the essential knowledge needed to be authentically well.

You will begin to have noticeable and remarkable gains in wellness rapidly. Probably more than you ever imagined. However, remember not to concern yourself with how fast you progress, and do not push yourself or rush. The wisdom and experiences that will lead you to additional wellness will become available to you automatically when you are ready, and no sooner. Relax, practice, and enjoy the exciting journey, every step of the way. The goal is the journey. In fact, it seems the more a person progresses, the more they realize how rich and vast this is, with always deeper self knowledge and wellness.

This final section will discuss some important obstacles you might encounter as you progress toward deeper wellness. Of course, the first barrier will be the discipline needed to practice. Then, after you get going, various other barriers to progress might emerge. Some will be tougher than others, and arguably no one issue will be more important than another. You might also encounter some challenges that are not discussed here. This discussion will cover conquering fear, maintaining clarity, and dealing with power. These challenges do not necessarily appear in this order, and will probably reappear from time to time.

If allowed, fear will stop you from having new and valuable experiences right from the start. Even the skill of relaxing deeply requires letting go of fear. In general, as you train and have new and unique experiences, welcome them without concern. This will allow you to develop more completely. Do not interpret the notion of conquering fear to mean that you should take unnecessary risks, or go out of your way to do what you fear. That would actually mean that fear gained the upper hand, and was controlling you by pushing you to prove your superiority. What you seek is to respect fear, for it is in many ways protective, yet not allow it to prevent you from fully experiencing what you desire or what you find before you.

Once you make some progress, with fear reasonably handled, you will find that you have better perceptual clarity, and an ability to experience and interact with the world in a more meaningful and authentic way. At this point, your challenge is maintaining this orientation. If you allow yourself to lose clarity you will revert back to a less fluid, less successful way because you will be interacting less deeply with yourself and the world. This could lead to a reduction in your personal effectiveness, and send you backward, reactivating fear again. To maintain clarity, you must continue to experience the world in your fluid state, as it comes to you naturally. You will thus behave in a manner that is more consistent with yourself and the world, and this interaction will be productive and beneficial.

As you continue to progress with wellness, after you have been interacting more effectively in the world, you will see that you have more power. You will experience things as they are, fearlessly interact with what is, and meet with success. Now a significant barrier to progress is the potentially destructive aspect of power. There are many ways that power can get the best of you. You might accidentally slip into self-destructive patterns of thinking and feeling, which do you more harm at this point, because you are a more powerful creator of your experiences. Or, you might begin to lose your ethical and moral compass, believing for example that you are better than others, and that you should gain at the expense of others. This separation of self from others could also begin to bring you down, as your self-importance becomes burdensome. As you gain power, be sure to maintain integrity and control your self-importance. Use your power judiciously, to do good for yourself and others. If you can get past the power barrier, you will become a much healthier person, moving farther down the self-development path than most, living life to its fullest, experiencing the world clearly, interacting with a purpose, and creating value in life for yourself and others.

Now at the end of our discussion, I want to wish you the very best. This book carries my vibrational intention to help you as much as possible. Please perform the practices you have learned, and revisit the book from time to time, for a vibrational boost and for insights you might have missed during this reading. Feel free also to send correspondence to the publisher about your experiences with Effortless Wellbeing™. Perhaps we will meet one day, at a seminar. I would like that.

Now, be authentically well! You deserve it!

Training
Journal

Summary of the Training Program

1. To gain a general sense of the program, read the entire book before beginning your training.

2. Implement all of the 'Critical Preliminary Notions' and as many ideas from the 'A Few More Critical Notions' section as possible.

3. Gain the 'Three Essential Skills', while keeping track of your practice in the training journal.

4. Once reasonably comfortable with the 'Three Essential Skills,' integrate them into the 'Four Essential Practices.' You no longer practice each skill in isolation. Continue using the training journal.

5. Revisit the book every so often for additional insights you might have missed, while maintaining your training as described.

6. Enjoy the training and be well!

The Journal Pages

The following journal pages will help you keep track of your progress. Two pages are devoted to each week. On the first page, you will track, with numerical values, what you did, for how long, and how you think it went. On the second page, you will write whatever you feel is important about the experiences you had during the week. There are 21 weeks worth of pages. Feel free to photocopy the journal template if you want more. Again, while journaling is said to have great value in itself, this journal is primarily here to help you gauge your progress, because it is often difficult to notice incremental changes without documentation. I recommend that you use the journal for this purpose. You will enjoy looking back.

Date: _____   Week Number: _____

Time in Minutes for each Day of Week

Skill Training	S	M	T	W	T	F	S
Breathing							
Calming Mind							
Relaxing Body							

Practice	S	M	T	W	T	F	S
Standing							
Sitting							
Lying on Back							
Moving							

Rate from 0 (not at all) to 10 (the most) the extent to which:

____You worked on eating, drinking, and sleeping.

____You were decent,with integrity.

____You remained calm and focused.

____You did supplemental exercises.

____You reduced self-importance and ego.

____You practiced acceptance and responsibility.

____You practiced desire and intention, without attachment.

____You felt energized and powerful.

____Your practices were effortless.

____Your practices reduced tension.

____Your practices produced inner silence.

____Your practice was enjoyable.

Date: _____   *Week Number:* _____

Write anything you want about the sensations and experiences you have had during this week. What if anything do you <u>not</u> want to say and why?

Write anything else that seems important to you. How's life? What do you desire? What is bothering you? What do you like about ... ?

118

Date: _____   Week Number: _____

Time in Minutes for each Day of Week

Skill Training	S	M	T	W	T	F	S
Breathing							
Calming Mind							
Relaxing Body							

Practice	S	M	T	W	T	F	S
Standing							
Sitting							
Lying on Back							
Moving							

Rate from 0 (not at all) to 10 (the most) the extent to which:

____You worked on eating, drinking, and sleeping.

____You were decent, with integrity.

____You remained calm and focused.

____You did supplemental exercises.

____You reduced self-importance and ego.

____You practiced acceptance and responsibility.

____You practiced desire and intention, without attachment.

____You felt energized and powerful.

____Your practices were effortless.

____Your practices reduced tension.

____Your practices produced inner silence.

____Your practice was enjoyable.

EFFORTLESS WELLBEING

Date: _____   *Week Number:* _____

Write anything you want about the sensations and experiences you have
had during this week. What if anything do you <u>not</u> want to say and why?

Write anything else that seems important to you. How's life? What do you
desire? What is bothering you? What do you like about ... ?

Date: _____   Week Number: _____

Time in Minutes for each Day of Week

Skill Training	S	M	T	W	T	F	S
Breathing							
Calming Mind							
Relaxing Body							

Practice	S	M	T	W	T	F	S
Standing							
Sitting							
Lying on Back							
Moving							

Rate from 0 (not at all) to 10 (the most) the extent to which:

_____ You worked on eating, drinking, and sleeping.

_____ You were decent, with integrity.

_____ You remained calm and focused.

_____ You did supplemental exercises.

_____ You reduced self-importance and ego.

_____ You practiced acceptance and responsibility.

_____ You practiced desire and intention, without attachment.

_____ You felt energized and powerful.

_____ Your practices were effortless.

_____ Your practices reduced tension.

_____ Your practices produced inner silence.

_____ Your practice was enjoyable.

EFFORTLESS WELLBEING

Date: _____   *Week Number:* _____

Write anything you want about the sensations and experiences you have had during this week. What if anything do you <u>not</u> want to say and why?

Write anything else that seems important to you. How's life? What do you desire? What is bothering you? What do you like about ... ?

Date: _____   Week Number: _____

Time in Minutes for each Day of Week

Skill Training	S	M	T	W	T	F	S
Breathing							
Calming Mind							
Relaxing Body							

Practice	S	M	T	W	T	F	S
Standing							
Sitting							
Lying on Back							
Moving							

Rate from 0 (not at all) to 10 (the most) the extent to which:

____You worked on eating, drinking, and sleeping.

____You were decent, with integrity.

____You remained calm and focused.

____You did supplemental exercises.

____You reduced self-importance and ego.

____You practiced acceptance and responsibility.

____You practiced desire and intention, without attachment.

____You felt energized and powerful.

____Your practices were effortless.

____Your practices reduced tension.

____Your practices produced inner silence.

____Your practice was enjoyable.

Date: _____   *Week Number:* _____

Write anything you want about the sensations and experiences you have had during this week. What if anything do you <u>not</u> want to say and why?

Write anything else that seems important to you. How's life? What do you desire? What is bothering you? What do you like about ... ?

Date: _____   Week Number: _____

Time in Minutes for each Day of Week

Skill Training	S	M	T	W	T	F	S
Breathing							
Calming Mind							
Relaxing Body							

Practice	S	M	T	W	T	F	S
Standing							
Sitting							
Lying on Back							
Moving							

Rate from 0 (not at all) to 10 (the most) the extent to which:

____You worked on eating, drinking, and sleeping.
____You were decent, with integrity.
____You remained calm and focused.
____You did supplemental exercises.
____You reduced self-importance and ego.
____You practiced acceptance and responsibility.
____You practiced desire and intention, without attachment.
____You felt energized and powerful.
____Your practices were effortless.
____Your practices reduced tension.
____Your practices produced inner silence.
____Your practice was enjoyable.

Date: _____   *Week Number:* _____

Write anything you want about the sensations and experiences you have had during this week. What if anything do you <u>not</u> want to say and why?

Write anything else that seems important to you. How's life? What do you desire? What is bothering you? What do you like about ... ?

Date: _____   Week Number: _____

Time in Minutes for each Day of Week

Skill Training	S	M	T	W	T	F	S
Breathing							
Calming Mind							
Relaxing Body							

Practice	S	M	T	W	T	F	S
Standing							
Sitting							
Lying on Back							
Moving							

Rate from 0 (not at all) to 10 (the most) the extent to which:

____You worked on eating, drinking, and sleeping.

____You were decent, with integrity.

____You remained calm and focused.

____You did supplemental exercises.

____You reduced self-importance and ego.

____You practiced acceptance and responsibility.

____You practiced desire and intention, without attachment.

____You felt energized and powerful.

____Your practices were effortless.

____Your practices reduced tension.

____Your practices produced inner silence.

____Your practice was enjoyable.

127

EFFORTLESS WELLBEING

Date: _____   *Week Number:* _____

Write anything you want about the sensations and experiences you have had during this week. What if anything do you <u>not</u> want to say and why?

Write anything else that seems important to you. How's life? What do you desire? What is bothering you? What do you like about ... ?

The Missing Ingredients for Authentic Wellness

Date: _____   Week Number: _____

Time in Minutes for each Day of Week

Skill Training	S	M	T	W	T	F	S
Breathing							
Calming Mind							
Relaxing Body							

Practice	S	M	T	W	T	F	S
Standing							
Sitting							
Lying on Back							
Moving							

Rate from 0 (not at all) to 10 (the most) the extent to which:

____You worked on eating, drinking, and sleeping.
____You were decent, with integrity.
____You remained calm and focused.
____You did supplemental exercises.
____You reduced self-importance and ego.
____You practiced acceptance and responsibility.
____You practiced desire and intention, without attachment.
____You felt energized and powerful.
____Your practices were effortless.
____Your practices reduced tension.
____Your practices produced inner silence.
____Your practice was enjoyable.

129

Date: _____   *Week Number:* _____

Write anything you want about the sensations and experiences you have had during this week. What if anything do you <u>not</u> want to say and why?

Write anything else that seems important to you. How's life? What do you desire? What is bothering you? What do you like about ... ?

Date: _____   Week Number: _____

	Time in Minutes for each Day of Week						
Skill Training	*S*	*M*	*T*	*W*	*T*	*F*	*S*
Breathing							
Calming Mind							
Relaxing Body							

Practice	*S*	*M*	*T*	*W*	*T*	*F*	*S*
Standing							
Sitting							
Lying on Back							
Moving							

Rate from 0 (not at all) to 10 (the most) the extent to which:

____You worked on eating, drinking, and sleeping.

____You were decent, with integrity.

____You remained calm and focused.

____You did supplemental exercises.

____You reduced self-importance and ego.

____You practiced acceptance and responsibility.

____You practiced desire and intention, without attachment.

____You felt energized and powerful.

____Your practices were effortless.

____Your practices reduced tension.

____Your practices produced inner silence.

____Your practice was enjoyable.

131

Date: _____   *Week Number:* _____

Write anything you want about the sensations and experiences you have had during this week. What if anything do you <u>not</u> want to say and why?

Write anything else that seems important to you. How's life? What do you desire? What is bothering you? What do you like about ... ?

Date: _____   Week Number: _____

Time in Minutes for each Day of Week

Skill Training	*S*	*M*	*T*	*W*	*T*	*F*	*S*
Breathing							
Calming Mind							
Relaxing Body							

Practice	*S*	*M*	*T*	*W*	*T*	*F*	*S*
Standing							
Sitting							
Lying on Back							
Moving							

Rate from 0 (not at all) to 10 (the most) the extent to which:

_____You worked on eating, drinking, and sleeping.

_____You were decent, with integrity.

_____You remained calm and focused.

_____You did supplemental exercises.

_____You reduced self-importance and ego.

_____You practiced acceptance and responsibility.

_____You practiced desire and intention, without attachment.

_____You felt energized and powerful.

_____Your practices were effortless.

_____Your practices reduced tension.

_____Your practices produced inner silence.

_____Your practice was enjoyable.

Date: _____   *Week Number:* _____

Write anything you want about the sensations and experiences you have had during this week. What if anything do you <u>not</u> want to say and why?

Write anything else that seems important to you. How's life? What do you desire? What is bothering you? What do you like about ... ?

Date: _____   Week Number: _____

Time in Minutes for each Day of Week

Skill Training	S	M	T	W	T	F	S
Breathing							
Calming Mind							
Relaxing Body							

Practice	S	M	T	W	T	F	S
Standing							
Sitting							
Lying on Back							
Moving							

Rate from 0 (not at all) to 10 (the most) the extent to which:

____You worked on eating, drinking, and sleeping.

____You were decent, with integrity.

____You remained calm and focused.

____You did supplemental exercises.

____You reduced self-importance and ego.

____You practiced acceptance and responsibility.

____You practiced desire and intention, without attachment.

____You felt energized and powerful.

____Your practices were effortless.

____Your practices reduced tension.

____Your practices produced inner silence.

____Your practice was enjoyable.

EFFORTLESS WELLBEING

Date: _____   *Week Number:* _____

Write anything you want about the sensations and experiences you have had during this week. What if anything do you <u>not</u> want to say and why?

Write anything else that seems important to you. How's life? What do you desire? What is bothering you? What do you like about ... ?

Date: _____   Week Number: _____

				Time in Minutes for each Day of Week				
Skill Training	S	M	T	W	T	F	S
Breathing							
Calming Mind							
Relaxing Body							

Practice	S	M	T	W	T	F	S
Standing							
Sitting							
Lying on Back							
Moving							

Rate from 0 (not at all) to 10 (the most) the extent to which:

_____ You worked on eating, drinking, and sleeping.

_____ You were decent, with integrity.

_____ You remained calm and focused.

_____ You did supplemental exercises.

_____ You reduced self-importance and ego.

_____ You practiced acceptance and responsibility.

_____ You practiced desire and intention, without attachment.

_____ You felt energized and powerful.

_____ Your practices were effortless.

_____ Your practices reduced tension.

_____ Your practices produced inner silence.

_____ Your practice was enjoyable.

Date: _____   *Week Number:* _____

Write anything you want about the sensations and experiences you have had during this week. What if anything do you <u>not</u> want to say and why?

Write anything else that seems important to you. How's life? What do you desire? What is bothering you? What do you like about ... ?

Date: _____   Week Number: _____

Time in Minutes for each Day of Week

Skill Training	S	M	T	W	T	F	S
Breathing							
Calming Mind							
Relaxing Body							

Practice	S	M	T	W	T	F	S
Standing							
Sitting							
Lying on Back							
Moving							

Rate from 0 (not at all) to 10 (the most) the extent to which:

_____You worked on eating, drinking, and sleeping.

_____You were decent, with integrity.

_____You remained calm and focused.

_____You did supplemental exercises.

_____You reduced self-importance and ego.

_____You practiced acceptance and responsibility.

_____You practiced desire and intention, without attachment.

_____You felt energized and powerful.

_____Your practices were effortless.

_____Your practices reduced tension.

_____Your practices produced inner silence.

_____Your practice was enjoyable.

Date: _____   *Week Number:* _____

Write anything you want about the sensations and experiences you have had during this week. What if anything do you <u>not</u> want to say and why?

Write anything else that seems important to you. How's life? What do you desire? What is bothering you? What do you like about ... ?

Date: _____   Week Number: _____

				Time in Minutes for each Day of Week				
Skill Training	S	M	T	W	T	F	S
Breathing							
Calming Mind							
Relaxing Body							

Practice	S	M	T	W	T	F	S
Standing							
Sitting							
Lying on Back							
Moving							

Rate from 0 (not at all) to 10 (the most) the extent to which:

_____ You worked on eating, drinking, and sleeping.

_____ You were decent, with integrity.

_____ You remained calm and focused.

_____ You did supplemental exercises.

_____ You reduced self-importance and ego.

_____ You practiced acceptance and responsibility.

_____ You practiced desire and intention, without attachment.

_____ You felt energized and powerful.

_____ Your practices were effortless.

_____ Your practices reduced tension.

_____ Your practices produced inner silence.

_____ Your practice was enjoyable.

Date: _____   *Week Number:* _____

Write anything you want about the sensations and experiences you have had during this week. What if anything do you <u>not</u> want to say and why?

Write anything else that seems important to you. How's life? What do you desire? What is bothering you? What do you like about ... ?

Date: _____   Week Number: _____

Time in Minutes for each Day of Week

Skill Training	S	M	T	W	T	F	S
Breathing							
Calming Mind							
Relaxing Body							

Practice	S	M	T	W	T	F	S
Standing							
Sitting							
Lying on Back							
Moving							

Rate from 0 (not at all) to 10 (the most) the extent to which:

____ You worked on eating, drinking, and sleeping.

____ You were decent, with integrity.

____ You remained calm and focused.

____ You did supplemental exercises.

____ You reduced self-importance and ego.

____ You practiced acceptance and responsibility.

____ You practiced desire and intention, without attachment.

____ You felt energized and powerful.

____ Your practices were effortless.

____ Your practices reduced tension.

____ Your practices produced inner silence.

____ Your practice was enjoyable.

EFFORTLESS WELLBEING

Date: _____   *Week Number:* _____

Write anything you want about the sensations and experiences you have had during this week. What if anything do you <u>not</u> want to say and why?

Write anything else that seems important to you. How's life? What do you desire? What is bothering you? What do you like about ... ?

Date: _____   Week Number: _____

Time in Minutes for each Day of Week

Skill Training	S	M	T	W	T	F	S
Breathing							
Calming Mind							
Relaxing Body							

Practice	S	M	T	W	T	F	S
Standing							
Sitting							
Lying on Back							
Moving							

Rate from 0 (not at all) to 10 (the most) the extent to which:

____You worked on eating, drinking, and sleeping.

____You were decent, with integrity.

____You remained calm and focused.

____You did supplemental exercises.

____You reduced self-importance and ego.

____You practiced acceptance and responsibility.

____You practiced desire and intention, without attachment.

____You felt energized and powerful.

____Your practices were effortless.

____Your practices reduced tension.

____Your practices produced inner silence.

____Your practice was enjoyable.

145

Date: _____   *Week Number:* _____

Write anything you want about the sensations and experiences you have had during this week. What if anything do you <u>not</u> want to say and why?

Write anything else that seems important to you. How's life? What do you desire? What is bothering you? What do you like about ... ?

Date: _____   Week Number: _____

Time in Minutes for each Day of Week

Skill Training	S	M	T	W	T	F	S
Breathing							
Calming Mind							
Relaxing Body							

Practice	S	M	T	W	T	F	S
Standing							
Sitting							
Lying on Back							
Moving							

Rate from 0 (not at all) to 10 (the most) the extent to which:

____You worked on eating, drinking, and sleeping.

____You were decent, with integrity.

____You remained calm and focused.

____You did supplemental exercises.

____You reduced self-importance and ego.

____You practiced acceptance and responsibility.

____You practiced desire and intention, without attachment.

____You felt energized and powerful.

____Your practices were effortless.

____Your practices reduced tension.

____Your practices produced inner silence.

____Your practice was enjoyable.

Date: _____   *Week Number:* _____

Write anything you want about the sensations and experiences you have had during this week. What if anything do you <u>not</u> want to say and why?

Write anything else that seems important to you. How's life? What do you desire? What is bothering you? What do you like about ... ?

Date: _____   Week Number: _____

Time in Minutes for each Day of Week

Skill Training	S	M	T	W	T	F	S
Breathing							
Calming Mind							
Relaxing Body							

Practice	S	M	T	W	T	F	S
Standing							
Sitting							
Lying on Back							
Moving							

Rate from 0 (not at all) to 10 (the most) the extent to which:

_____You worked on eating, drinking, and sleeping.

_____You were decent, with integrity.

_____You remained calm and focused.

_____You did supplemental exercises.

_____You reduced self-importance and ego.

_____You practiced acceptance and responsibility.

_____You practiced desire and intention, without attachment.

_____You felt energized and powerful.

_____Your practices were effortless.

_____Your practices reduced tension.

_____Your practices produced inner silence.

_____Your practice was enjoyable.

Date: _____   *Week Number:* _____

Write anything you want about the sensations and experiences you have had during this week. What if anything do you <u>not</u> want to say and why?

Write anything else that seems important to you. How's life? What do you desire? What is bothering you? What do you like about ... ?

Date: _____   Week Number: _____

Time in Minutes for each Day of Week

Skill Training	S	M	T	W	T	F	S
Breathing							
Calming Mind							
Relaxing Body							

Practice	S	M	T	W	T	F	S
Standing							
Sitting							
Lying on Back							
Moving							

Rate from 0 (not at all) to 10 (the most) the extent to which:

____You worked on eating, drinking, and sleeping.

____You were decent, with integrity.

____You remained calm and focused.

____You did supplemental exercises.

____You reduced self-importance and ego.

____You practiced acceptance and responsibility.

____You practiced desire and intention, without attachment.

____You felt energized and powerful.

____Your practices were effortless.

____Your practices reduced tension.

____Your practices produced inner silence.

____Your practice was enjoyable.

Date: _____   *Week Number:* _____

Write anything you want about the sensations and experiences you have had during this week. What if anything do you <u>not</u> want to say and why?

Write anything else that seems important to you. How's life? What do you desire? What is bothering you? What do you like about ... ?

Date: _____   Week Number: _____

Time in Minutes for each Day of Week

Skill Training	S	M	T	W	T	F	S
Breathing							
Calming Mind							
Relaxing Body							

Practice	S	M	T	W	T	F	S
Standing							
Sitting							
Lying on Back							
Moving							

Rate from 0 (not at all) to 10 (the most) the extent to which:

____You worked on eating, drinking, and sleeping.

____You were decent, with integrity.

____You remained calm and focused.

____You did supplemental exercises.

____You reduced self-importance and ego.

____You practiced acceptance and responsibility.

____You practiced desire and intention, without attachment.

____You felt energized and powerful.

____Your practices were effortless.

____Your practices reduced tension.

____Your practices produced inner silence.

____Your practice was enjoyable.

EFFORTLESS WELLBEING

Date: _____   *Week Number:* _____

Write anything you want about the sensations and experiences you have had during this week. What if anything do you <u>not</u> want to say and why?

Write anything else that seems important to you. How's life? What do you desire? What is bothering you? What do you like about ... ?

Date: _____   Week Number: _____

<u>Time in Minutes for each Day of Week</u>

Skill Training	S	M	T	W	T	F	S
Breathing							
Calming Mind							
Relaxing Body							

Practice	S	M	T	W	T	F	S
Standing							
Sitting							
Lying on Back							
Moving							

Rate from 0 (not at all) to 10 (the most) the extent to which:

____You worked on eating, drinking, and sleeping.

____You were decent, with integrity.

____You remained calm and focused.

____You did supplemental exercises.

____You reduced self-importance and ego.

____You practiced acceptance and responsibility.

____You practiced desire and intention, without attachment.

____You felt energized and powerful.

____Your practices were effortless.

____Your practices reduced tension.

____Your practices produced inner silence.

____Your practice was enjoyable.

Date: _____   *Week Number:* _____

Write anything you want about the sensations and experiences you have had during this week. What if anything do you <u>not</u> want to say and why?

Write anything else that seems important to you. How's life? What do you desire? What is bothering you? What do you like about ... ?

Date: _____   Week Number: _____

Time in Minutes for each Day of Week

Skill Training	S	M	T	W	T	F	S
Breathing							
Calming Mind							
Relaxing Body							

Practice	S	M	T	W	T	F	S
Standing							
Sitting							
Lying on Back							
Moving							

Rate from 0 (not at all) to 10 (the most) the extent to which:

____You worked on eating, drinking, and sleeping.

____You were decent, with integrity.

____You remained calm and focused.

____You did supplemental exercises.

____You reduced self-importance and ego.

____You practiced acceptance and responsibility.

____You practiced desire and intention, without attachment.

____You felt energized and powerful.

____Your practices were effortless.

____Your practices reduced tension.

____Your practices produced inner silence.

____Your practice was enjoyable.

Date: _____   *Week Number:* _____

Write anything you want about the sensations and experiences you have had during this week. What if anything do you <u>not</u> want to say and why?

Write anything else that seems important to you. How's life? What do you desire? What is bothering you? What do you like about ... ?

About the Author

Appreciated for his uniquely straightforward, integrative, and effective style, Evan Finer brings extensive knowledge, experience, and skill to the endeavor of transmitting the principles and practices for effortless wellbeing. In addition to writing, he teaches individuals and groups. People, with various skill levels and backgrounds, consistently benefit from his generous guidance. In addition to drawing from his diligent practice of wellness disciplines since the late 1970s, Evan has a rigorous academic background, which helped him gain quality tools for the researching, developing, and communicating of his ideas (B.A., Northwestern University; M.A., Loyola University Chicago; satisfied curiosity in thousands of hours of Ph.D. level training). Evan lives in the northern suburbs of Chicago, Illinois, with his wife, Ellen, and daughter, Erin.

Additional Training Opportunities

Here are some ways you can supplement your Effortless Wellbeing™ training:

Audio Book with Exercises: The author reads the text of the book in its entirety. Also contains audio guidance, with the author, through several exercise and practice sessions. This is a very helpful product. Contact your local bookseller (reference ISBN 0-9743077-1-8), or contact Wellbeing Resources to get the audio program.

Seminar Learning Format: Evan Finer conducts seminars for the Effortless Wellbeing™ system. If you find working with his book helpful, you will want to look into registering for this remarkable seminar. Contact Wellbeing Resources or visit our website www.wellbeingresources.com for more information.